The woman of Enneagram 3: Love marriage success edition

Enneagram For Women, Volume 3

Maria Rondon

Published by Maria Rondon, 2024.

THE WOMAN OF ENNEAGRAM 3

THE WOMAN OF ENNEAGRAM 3: LOVE MARRIAGE SUCCESS EDITION

First edition. March 28, 2024.

Copyright © 2024 Maria Rondon.

ISBN: 979-8227306043

Written by Maria Rondon.

SANS SERIF

CONTENT
The Enneagram and the Power of Achievement:

- A historical overview of the Enneagram and its relevance to self-knowledge, specifically for Enneagram Threes.
- How the Enneagram can be a tool for understanding your core motivations, fears, and desires for success.
- The Three's Journey:

- From Driven to Fulfilled: This section will explore how self-understanding can empower Type Three women in various aspects of their lives, including relationships, career, and personal growth.
- Moving Beyond the Image: This section will delve into the potential challenges Threes face with self-worth, authenticity, and vulnerability.

Chapter 1: Achieving Success on Your Terms

- Goal Setting for Threes: Strategies for setting meaningful goals that align with your values and inner desires, not just external validation.
- Building Confidence from Within: Techniques for developing a strong sense of self-worth that goes beyond accomplishments.
- Subtype Spotlight: How Self-Preservation, Social, and Sexual Threes Approach Success: Analyzing how subtypes influence how Threes define and pursue success.

Chapter 2: Cultivating Healthy Relationships

- The Power of Authenticity in Connections: Strategies for building genuine connections based on vulnerability and emotional honesty.
- Managing Competition in Relationships: Techniques for fostering collaboration and support within your relationships, both personal and professional.

Chapter 3: Finding Balance and Well-being

- From Workaholic to Balanced: Strategies for maintaining a healthy work-life balance and preventing burnout.
- Beyond the "Go-Getter" Mentality: Techniques for practicing self-care and relaxation to support your physical and mental well-being.

Chapter 4: Embracing Your Full Potential

- Unmasking Your Passions: Exercises to help you discover your intrinsic motivations and passions beyond external validation.
- The Power of Vulnerability and Growth: Techniques for embracing your vulnerabilities as a source of strength and personal growth.

Chapter 5: Women and Leadership

- Leading with Authenticity: Strategies for leading with confidence while staying true to your values and personality.
- Building Strong Teams: Techniques for fostering collaboration and motivation within your team.

Chapter 6: Exploring Your Wings

- Understanding the Influences of Type Four and Type Two: A section dedicated to exploring how the wings (Type 3w4 and Type 3w2) influence personality, strengths, and challenges of Threes.
- Growth and Integration: Moving Towards Health: Examining how 3s integrate towards Type 6 (in growth) and disintegrate towards Type 9 (under stress), and offering strategies for managing these movements.

The Enneagram and the Power of Achievement:

The Enneagram and the Power of Achievement: A Historical Overview and Its Relevance to Self-Knowledge for Enneagram Type 3s

The Enneagram, an ancient and complex system of personality typology, offers invaluable insights into human behavior and motivations, serving as a profound tool for self-discovery and personal growth. Its historical roots, shrouded in mystery, span back to ancient spiritual and philosophical traditions, suggesting a rich tapestry of wisdom that has evolved over centuries. This chapter explores the historical evolution of the Enneagram and its particular significance for individuals who identify with Type 3, known as The Achiever, in their quest for self-knowledge and personal achievement.

The Enneagram's Ancient Origins

The origins of the Enneagram are believed to date back to antiquity, with its foundational elements rooted in various spiritual and philosophical traditions across the world. The symbol itself, a nine-pointed figure, captures the essence of universal laws and truths, a concept revered by ancient thinkers such as the Pythagoreans and Neoplatonists in Greece. These early mentions highlight the Enneagram's symbolic significance and its potential as a tool for understanding the cosmic order and the human soul.

The Development of the Enneagram

The modern interpretation of the Enneagram, particularly its application to personality typology, owes much to the pioneering work of George Gurdjieff, Peter Ouspensky, and their successors. Gurdjieff, a spiritual teacher of Greek-Armenian descent, is credited with introducing the Enneagram symbol to the West, presenting it as a window into human psychology and the dynamics of transformation. Ouspensky further popularized Gurdjieff's teachings, emphasizing the Enneagram's role in self-observation and inner work.

The latter half of the 20th century saw a resurgence in the Enneagram's popularity, with scholars such as Claudio Naranjo, Oscar Ichazo, and Helen Palmer expanding upon its psychological dimensions. Their contributions enriched the Enneagram system with a deeper understanding of the nine personality types, including Type 3, and their distinctive pathways to growth and integration.

Enneagram Type 3: The Achiever

Type 3s, or The Achievers, are characterized by their drive for success, adaptability, and innate desire for recognition. They embody the principles of excellence and efficiency, striving to be exemplary in their endeavors and to attain esteemed positions within their communities. However, this drive can also lead to challenges, such as losing touch with their authentic selves in the pursuit of external validation and achievement.

The Enneagram's Relevance to Type 3s

For Type 3s, the Enneagram serves as a mirror reflecting both their strengths and vulnerabilities. It provides a framework for understanding their core motivations—the desire to be valued and admired—and the fears that accompany their pursuit of success. By engaging with the Enneagram, Type 3s can embark on a journey of self-exploration, uncovering the deeper values and personal truths that lie beneath their achievements.

Strategies for Growth and Integration

The path to growth for Type 3s involves embracing authenticity and cultivating a sense of worth that is independent of their accomplishments. Practices such as mindfulness, self-reflection, and the pursuit of activities that align with their true passions can foster a deeper connection to their inner selves. Additionally, exploring the movements towards health (integration towards Type Six) and under stress (disintegration towards Type Nine) can offer Type 3s strategies for managing challenges and harnessing their potential for personal and spiritual growth.

The Enneagram, with its ancient roots and modern interpretations, offers Type 3s a powerful tool for achieving self-knowledge and personal transformation. By understanding the historical context and applying the insights gained from their Enneagram type, Type 3 women can navigate the complexities of their personalities, embracing both their achievements and their vulnerabilities. This chapter not only honors the rich history of the Enneagram but also illuminates the path towards authenticity, fulfillment, and true achievement for Enneagram Type 3s.

The Enneagram and the Power of Achievement: Understanding Your Core Motivations, Fears, and Desires for Success

The Enneagram, a tool of ancient origin with profound implications for self-discovery, offers invaluable insights into the intricate dynamics of personality and personal development. For women who identify as Type 3, known as The Achiever, the Enneagram provides a lens through which to view their core motivations, fears, and the intricate weave of desires that fuel their pursuit of success. This chapter explores how the Enneagram, as a guide to self-knowledge, can help Type 3 women navigate the path to authentic achievement and fulfillment.

Core Motivations of Type 3s

At the heart of Type 3's drive is the desire to be esteemed and recognized for their accomplishments. This longing stems not from vanity but from a deep-seated need to feel valuable and worthy. The Enneagram illuminates this fundamental motivation, offering Type 3s a mirror to understand why achievement feels so critical to their sense of self. Acknowledging this need can be the first step towards embracing a more balanced approach to success, one that honors both their achievements and inherent worth.

Fears of Type 3s

The flip side of the Achiever's ambition is the fear of failure and the accompanying dread of worthlessness. This fear can drive Type 3s to relentlessly pursue success, at times at the expense of their authenticity and emotional well-being. The Enneagram sheds light on this fear, encouraging Type 3s to confront and work through it. Recognizing that their value does not diminish with setbacks or failures is crucial for Type 3s to develop resilience and a healthier relationship with success.

Desires for Success

Type 3s harbor a complex array of desires related to success. Beyond recognition and accolades, they seek to make a meaningful impact and to embody the ideals of excellence and efficiency. The Enneagram helps Type 3s to dissect these desires, differentiating between those that truly resonate with their core values and those influenced by external expectations. This discernment is key to pursuing success that is not only visible externally but also deeply fulfilling.

Strategies for Authentic Achievement

Self-Reflection: Regular self-reflection can help Type 3s stay aligned with their true motivations and values, preventing them from losing themselves in the pursuit of external validation.

Balancing Action with Contemplation: While action is the natural domain of Type 3s, integrating practices of contemplation, such as meditation or journaling, can provide the space for inner growth and authenticity.

Embracing Vulnerability: Vulnerability is a strength for Type 3s. Allowing themselves to be seen, with their imperfections and uncertainties, can lead to deeper connections and a more authentic expression of success.

Celebrating the Journey: Recognizing the value in the process, not just the outcome, helps Type 3s appreciate their growth, resilience, and the richness of their experiences, beyond the achievements.

Moving Beyond the Image: Challenges with Self-Worth, Authenticity, and Vulnerability for Type 3 Women

The journey of Enneagram Type 3 women, often characterized by the pursuit of achievement and recognition, brings with it the challenge of navigating the complex terrain of self-worth, authenticity, and vulnerability. These challenges, deeply embedded in the psyche of Type 3s, can act as barriers to true fulfillment and personal growth. This section explores these issues and offers insights into how Type 3 women can move beyond the image they present to the world, towards a more authentic and vulnerable self.

Self-Worth Tied to Achievements

For many Type 3 women, self-worth is intricately tied to their accomplishments and the recognition they receive from others. This connection can create a relentless drive for success, where self-esteem is constantly at the mercy of external validation. The Enneagram illuminates this pattern, highlighting the need for Type 3s to detach their sense of value from their achievements and to recognize their inherent worth, irrespective of performance.

The Challenge of Authenticity

The desire to be seen as successful and competent can lead Type 3s to adopt a chameleon-like ability to adapt and excel in various roles. While this adaptability is a strength, it can also lead to a disconnection from their true selves, as the image presented to the world may not fully align with their authentic desires and values. The journey towards authenticity involves a conscious effort to connect with and express their genuine selves, even at the risk of not meeting perceived expectations.

Vulnerability as Strength

Vulnerability is often seen as antithetical to the Type 3's image of strength and competence. Yet, it is in embracing vulnerability that Type 3s can find true strength and connection. Opening up about fears, failures, and uncertainties can be particularly challenging for Type 3 women, who might worry that such admissions could undermine their image. However, vulnerability fosters deeper relationships and self-acceptance, allowing Type 3s to experience the richness of human connection beyond achievements.

Strategies for Overcoming Challenges

Reflect on Core Values: Type 3 women can benefit from reflecting on their core values and aligning their goals with these deeper principles, rather than pursuing success for external validation.

Practice Mindfulness: Mindfulness practices can help Type 3s stay connected to their present experience and feelings, reducing the compulsion to constantly strive and achieve.

Embrace Failure as Growth: Viewing failure as an opportunity for growth and learning can help Type 3s detach their self-worth from their successes and embrace the journey with all its ups and downs.

Seek Authentic Connections: Cultivating relationships where authenticity and vulnerability are valued can provide a supportive environment for Type 3s to express their true selves.

Chapter 1:

Achieving Success on Your Terms

Goal Setting for Threes: Strategies for Setting Meaningful Goals That Align with Your Values and Inner Desires, Not Just External Validation

For Enneagram Type 3 women, known as The Achievers, the quest for success is often a defining aspect of their journey. However, true fulfillment comes not from the accolades and achievements recognized by the world but from pursuing goals that resonate deeply with personal values and inner desires. This chapter explores strategies for Type 3 women to set meaningful goals, ensuring that their path to success is authentic and aligned with who they truly are, beyond the veneer of external validation.

Identifying Your Core Values

The foundation of meaningful goal setting begins with a clear understanding of your core values. These are the principles that guide your decisions, shape your beliefs, and ultimately, define what success means to you. For Type 3s, this introspective process involves peeling back the layers of societal expectations and the desire to impress, to uncover the values that genuinely resonate with their true self.

Strategy: Dedicate time to self-reflection through journaling or meditation, focusing on questions that probe deeper into your motivations, such as "What achievements make me feel the most fulfilled?" or "When do I feel most authentically myself?" This exploration can reveal the values that should guide your goal-setting process.

Aligning Goals with Inner Desires

Once you've identified your core values, the next step is to align your goals with these principles. For Type 3s, the challenge is to ensure that goals are not solely influenced by external markers of success but are deeply connected to what brings personal satisfaction and joy.

Strategy: For each goal you consider, ask yourself whether it serves your core values and fulfills an inner desire, not just an external expectation. This alignment ensures that your pursuit of success is meaningful and rewarding on a personal level.

Setting Balanced Goals

Achievers excel in professional and competitive realms, but setting goals that encompass all aspects of life, including personal growth, relationships, and self-care, is crucial. A holistic approach to goal setting allows Type 3s to nurture their well-being and maintain balance, preventing burnout and ensuring that success is sustainable and enriching.

Strategy: Create goals in various life domains, not just career or achievement-oriented areas. Consider setting goals related to emotional intelligence, cultivating deeper relationships, and personal hobbies or interests that bring you joy.

Embracing Vulnerability in Goal Pursuit

For Type 3s, vulnerability can be challenging, especially when it comes to acknowledging fears and uncertainties associated with pursuing deeply personal goals. However, embracing vulnerability is a strength that can lead to greater authenticity and connection with others.

Strategy: Share your goals and the values behind them with trusted friends or mentors. This act of vulnerability not only strengthens relationships but also reinforces your commitment to pursuing goals that are true to yourself.

Celebrating Progress and Learning from Setbacks

The journey toward achieving meaningful goals is as important as the destination. Type 3s can benefit from celebrating progress, no matter how small, and viewing setbacks not as failures but as opportunities for growth and learning.

Strategy: Regularly reflect on the progress made towards your goals, acknowledging the effort and growth along the way. When faced with setbacks, assess what can be learned from the experience and how it can inform future endeavors.

Enneagram Type 3 women, setting meaningful goals that align with core values and inner desires offers a path to authentic success and fulfillment. By focusing on what truly matters to them, beyond the allure of external validation, Type 3s can achieve success on their terms, enriched by a sense of personal satisfaction and growth. This chapter guides Type 3s in embracing a goal-setting approach that honors their values, nurtures their well-being, and celebrates their unique journey toward achieving meaningful success.

Building Confidence from Within: Techniques for Developing a Strong Sense of Self-Worth That Goes Beyond Accomplishments

For Enneagram Type 3 women, known for their drive, ambition, and the pursuit of success, building confidence that is rooted in internal validation rather than external achievements is a transformative journey.

This chapter delves into practical techniques that empower Type 3 women to cultivate a deep-seated sense of self-worth, independent of their accomplishments, and aligns with the ancient wisdom of the Enneagram for self-knowledge and growth.

Embracing Your Authentic Self

At the core of building genuine self-worth is the embrace of one's authentic self. For Type 3s, this means recognizing and valuing the person behind the achievements.

Technique: Begin with introspection. Allocate time for self-reflection to explore your thoughts, feelings, and motivations. Ask yourself what you value most about who you are, not just what you do. Practices such as journaling or meditation can facilitate this self-discovery, helping you to connect with your true essence beyond the roles and titles you may hold.

Cultivating Self-Compassion

Self-compassion is critical in developing a strong sense of self-worth. It involves treating oneself with the same kindness, care, and understanding that one would offer to a good friend.

Technique: Practice mindfulness to become aware of negative self-talk or critical inner dialogues. When you notice harsh self-criticism, intentionally shift your perspective and speak to yourself with compassion and empathy. Remind yourself of your humanity—that making mistakes and experiencing setbacks is a part of growth.

Recognizing Intrinsic Value

Understanding that your worth is inherent and not contingent on your successes or failures is fundamental for Type 3s.

Technique: Create a list of qualities and attributes you appreciate about yourself that are unrelated to achievements. These could include being a good listener, your sense of humor, or your ability to empathize with others. Regularly review and add to this list to reinforce the understanding that your value is not tied to productivity or accomplishments.

Setting Boundaries for Balanced Achievement

Setting healthy boundaries around work and achievement is essential for Type 3s to prevent self-worth from becoming overly tied to external validation.

Technique: Learn to say no to commitments that do not align with your core values or that compromise your well-being. Establish clear work-life boundaries to ensure you have time for self-care, relationships, and activities that bring you joy and fulfillment outside of your achievements.

Fostering Connections Based on Authenticity

Relationships grounded in authenticity, rather than the mutual exchange of achievements, can significantly enhance a sense of self-worth.

Technique: Seek and nurture relationships with individuals who value you for who you are, not just what you can accomplish. Be open and vulnerable in your interactions, allowing your true self to be seen and appreciated.

developing a strong sense of self-worth that transcends achievements is both a challenge and an opportunity for profound personal growth. By embracing authenticity, practicing self-compassion, recognizing intrinsic value, setting healthy boundaries, and fostering genuine connections, Type 3s can build confidence from within. This inner confidence not only enriches their sense of self but also enhances their capacity for achieving success on their own terms, guided by the timeless insights of the Enneagram.

Subtype Spotlight: How Self-Preservation, Social, and Sexual Threes Approach Success

Within the Enneagram Type 3 demographic, known as The Achievers, variations in how success is defined and pursued can be attributed to their subtype: Self-Preservation, Social, or Sexual (One-to-One). This chapter explores the nuances of each subtype, offering insights into their distinct approaches to achieving success, guided by the rich historical and philosophical foundations of the Enneagram.

Self-Preservation 3s: The Security Seeker

Self-Preservation Threes are driven by a need for security and stability, which significantly influences their definition of success. For them, success is often measured in terms of material security, financial prosperity, and the establishment of a stable and comfortable lifestyle. They are adept at adapting to societal norms and expectations, often excelling in traditional careers that promise security and advancement.

Strategies for Success: For Self-Preservation Threes, setting realistic financial goals and prioritizing tasks that build towards long-term stability can be effective. Cultivating patience and recognizing the value of incremental progress towards achieving security can enhance their sense of accomplishment and fulfillment.

Social Threes: The Status Seeker

Social Threes are motivated by the desire for recognition, prestige, and social status. They are highly aware of societal hierarchies and often pursue success in fields that offer visibility and acknowledgment from their community and peers. Their definition of success is closely tied to their social standing and the roles they play within groups or organizations.

Strategies for Success: For Social Threes, networking and building strategic relationships can be key to advancing their goals. However, it's also important for them to cultivate authenticity in their interactions and to pursue achievements that resonate with their true values, not just those that offer external validation.

Sexual (One-to-One) 3s: The Intimacy Seeker

Sexual or One-to-One Threes are characterized by their focus on personal connections and achievements that enhance their intimate relationships. Their approach to success often involves excelling in areas that allow them to stand out to those they are close to or wish to impress on a more personal level. They are passionate and driven, with a desire for success that is both deeply personal and intertwined with their relationships.

Strategies for Success: For Sexual Threes, integrating personal passions with their pursuits can lead to more fulfilling achievements. Focusing on goals that not only bring personal satisfaction but also deepen connections with loved ones can provide a balanced approach to success.

Understanding the influence of subtypes on Enneagram Type 3 women offers valuable insights into their diverse paths to success. Whether driven by the need for security, status, or intimacy, each subtype brings a unique perspective to the pursuit of achievement. By recognizing and honoring their subtype-specific motivations and challenges, Type 3 women can tailor their strategies for success, ensuring their goals align with their deepest desires and values. This nuanced approach, rooted in the ancient wisdom of the Enneagram, empowers Type 3s to achieve success on their terms, blending self-knowledge with authentic achievement.

Chapter 2:

Cultivating Healthy Relationships

The Power of Authenticity in Connections: Strategies for Building Genuine Connections Based on Vulnerability and Emotional Honesty

In the realm of relationships, authenticity serves as the cornerstone for deep, meaningful connections. For Enneagram Type 3 women, known for their drive for success and tendency to adapt their persona to meet expectations, embracing vulnerability and emotional honesty can be particularly transformative. This chapter delves into strategies that empower Type 3 women to forge genuine connections, shedding the mask of achievement to reveal their true selves.

Embracing Vulnerability

Vulnerability is often perceived as a weakness, especially for those who strive to maintain an image of success and competence. However, it is in vulnerability that true strength lies, allowing for authentic connections to flourish.

Strategy: Begin by identifying safe spaces and relationships where you can express your feelings, doubts, and fears without judgment. Practice sharing your true thoughts and emotions, even if it feels uncomfortable at first. Remember, vulnerability fosters deeper understanding and connection, making it a powerful tool for strengthening relationships.

Cultivating Emotional Honesty

Emotional honesty involves being truthful about your feelings with yourself and others. It requires acknowledging and expressing a range of emotions, not just those deemed acceptable or positive.

Strategy: Develop a habit of regular self-reflection to understand your emotions better. Use journaling or mindfulness techniques to explore your feelings and their origins. When communicating with others, strive to express your emotions honestly and clearly, using "I feel" statements to own your feelings and encourage open dialogue.

Building Trust through Authenticity

Trust is the foundation of any strong relationship, and it is built on consistency, reliability, and authenticity. For Type 3 women, living authentically means aligning actions with true values and desires, rather than performing roles that garner approval.

Strategy: Reflect on what authenticity means to you and how it aligns with your core values. Make conscious choices that reflect your true self, and communicate openly about your values and beliefs with others. Trust that those who value you will appreciate your authenticity and that genuine connections are based on mutual respect and understanding.

Navigating the Fear of Rejection

The fear of rejection or disapproval can be a significant barrier to authenticity for Type 3s. Overcoming this fear involves accepting that not all relationships will thrive on vulnerability but recognizing that those that do are invaluable.

Strategy: Focus on the quality of relationships, not the quantity. Embrace the idea that being authentic may not please everyone, but it will attract and deepen connections with those who truly resonate with your genuine self. Remember, rejection is not a reflection of your worth but a sign of misalignment in values or needs.

the journey towards cultivating healthy relationships anchored in authenticity, vulnerability, and emotional honesty is both challenging and rewarding. By embracing these strategies, Type 3s can unlock the power of genuine connections, allowing for relationships that offer mutual growth, support, and fulfillment. This chapter underscores the significance of shedding societal expectations to reveal one's true self, fostering connections that are enriching and authentic. In doing so, Type 3 women can achieve a profound sense of belonging and acceptance, finding success not just in achievements, but in the rich tapestry of meaningful relationships built on the solid foundation of authenticity.

Managing Competition in Relationships: Techniques for Fostering Collaboration and Support Within Your Relationships, Both Personal and Professional

For Enneagram Type 3 women, who are naturally ambitious and driven towards success, the competitive instinct can sometimes seep into their personal and professional relationships. While a healthy level of competition can spur motivation and growth, an overemphasis on competing can hinder the development of supportive, collaborative connections. This chapter explores techniques designed to help Type 3 women balance their competitive nature with a collaborative spirit, enhancing the quality of their relationships and fostering environments where support and mutual success flourish.

Acknowledging the Role of Competition

The first step in managing competition within relationships is acknowledging its presence and understanding its impact. For Type 3s, competition can be a motivating force, but when unchecked, it may lead to conflicts, misunderstandings, or feelings of isolation.

Technique: Reflect on instances where competition has influenced your interactions. Ask yourself whether these competitive impulses have served to uplift or if they have unintentionally created distance or tension between you and others. This introspection can pave the way for more mindful engagement with your competitive tendencies.

Shifting Focus from Winning to Collaborating

Reframing how success is viewed can significantly impact the dynamics of your relationships. Instead of perceiving success as a zero-sum game where one's gain is another's loss, consider success as a collaborative effort where all parties can thrive.

Technique: Practice viewing achievements through a lens of collective success. In professional settings, encourage teamwork by setting shared goals. In personal relationships, celebrate the successes of others as if they were your own, reinforcing the idea that one person's win can be a victory for the entire group or relationship.

Developing Empathy and Understanding

Empathy plays a crucial role in transforming competitive relationships into supportive ones. By genuinely seeking to understand the perspectives, goals, and challenges of others, Type 3s can foster deeper connections and collaborative spirit.

Technique: Engage in active listening during conversations, focusing fully on the other person without planning your response or thinking about your own experiences. Ask questions that encourage others to share more about their thoughts and feelings, and reflect back what you hear to ensure understanding and show that you value their perspective.

Celebrating Others' Successes

A hallmark of healthy, non-competitive relationships is the ability to celebrate the achievements of others genuinely. For Type 3s, this may require a conscious effort to overcome any feelings of envy or competitiveness.

Technique: Make a habit of recognizing and applauding the successes of friends, family, and colleagues. Express your congratulations verbally, write a note, or celebrate their achievements through small gestures. These acts of genuine goodwill can reinforce a sense of collaboration and mutual support.

Setting Boundaries Around Competition

Finally, setting clear boundaries around competitive behavior can help maintain the health and integrity of your relationships. This involves recognizing when competitive instincts are helpful and when they may be harmful.

Technique: When you notice competitive feelings arising, pause to assess their appropriateness for the situation. If competition is not beneficial, consciously choose to step back and adopt a more collaborative approach. Communicate with others about your intentions to foster supportive interactions, inviting them to join you in creating a more collaborative environment.

Enneagram Type 3 women, balancing the natural inclination towards competition with a commitment to collaboration and support can significantly enhance the quality of their relationships. By employing these techniques, Type 3s can nurture environments where everyone is encouraged to grow and succeed together, transforming competition into a force for collective achievement and deeper connection. This chapter not only offers practical strategies for managing competition but also highlights the importance of empathy, celebration of others, and the conscious cultivation of collaborative spirit in building healthy, fulfilling relationships.

Chapter 3:

Finding Balance and Well-being

From Workaholic to Balanced: Strategies for Maintaining a Healthy Work-Life Balance and Preventing Burnout

In a culture that often equates success with relentless work and achievement, Enneagram Type 3 women, also known as The Achievers, can find themselves on a fast track to burnout. Their intrinsic drive for success and recognition makes them susceptible to tipping the scales too far towards work, at the expense of personal well-being and life outside of professional pursuits. This chapter is dedicated to strategies that help Type 3 women find a more balanced approach, ensuring they maintain their drive while also nurturing their health and personal relationships.

Prioritizing Self-Care

Self-care is not indulgence but a necessity for maintaining energy, focus, and emotional well-being. For Type 3s, integrating self-care into their daily routines can be a game-changer.

Strategy: Schedule self-care activities with the same importance as work meetings. Whether it's a morning meditation, a midday walk, or an evening hobby, make these non-negotiable appointments with yourself.

Recognize that self-care directly contributes to your productivity and success by recharging your mental and physical batteries.

Setting Clear Boundaries

Type 3 women often blur the lines between work and personal life, which can lead to burnout. Setting clear boundaries is crucial for maintaining balance.

Strategy: Define specific work hours and stick to them, making an effort to completely disconnect from work outside of these times. Communicate these boundaries to colleagues, clients, and family members. Use technology to your advantage by setting "Do Not Disturb" hours on devices to safeguard your personal time.

Embracing Quality Over Quantity

In their quest for achievement, Type 3s might find themselves juggling multiple projects or commitments. However, spreading oneself too thin can dilute the quality of work and lead to burnout.

Strategy: Practice saying no to opportunities that do not align with your core goals or values. Focus on a few key projects or goals that are most meaningful to you and where you can make the biggest impact. This selective approach allows for deeper engagement and satisfaction in your work.

Cultivating Meaningful Relationships

Social connections and meaningful relationships are essential for emotional well-being and can provide a counterbalance to work-focused tendencies.

Strategy: Make intentional efforts to spend quality time with friends and family. Plan regular activities that encourage connection and relaxation. Being present in these moments helps reinforce the value of relationships outside of professional achievements.

Mindfulness and Reflection

Mindfulness practices can help Type 3s stay connected to their inner selves and their true motivations, preventing them from getting lost in the pursuit of external validation.

Strategy: Incorporate mindfulness practices into your daily routine, such as meditation, deep breathing exercises, or mindful walking. Regular reflection through journaling can also offer insights into your feelings and behaviors, helping you stay aligned with your true self.

Enneagram Type 3 women, achieving balance between their professional ambitions and personal well-being is both a challenge and an opportunity for growth. By prioritizing self-care, setting clear boundaries, focusing on meaningful projects, cultivating relationships, and embracing mindfulness, Type 3s can maintain their drive for success while ensuring they remain healthy, fulfilled, and balanced. This chapter not only offers practical strategies for achieving this balance but also highlights the importance of self-awareness and personal growth in the journey of The Achiever, enabling them to thrive in all aspects of life

Beyond the "Go-Getter" Mentality: Techniques for Practicing Self-Care and Relaxation to Support Your Physical and Mental Well-being

For Enneagram Type 3 women, the relentless pursuit of success and the drive to excel can often come at the expense of their physical and mental well-being. Known for their "go-getter" mentality, Type 3s may find it challenging to prioritize self-care and relaxation amidst their ambitious endeavors. This chapter offers techniques specifically tailored for Type 3 women, encouraging them to embrace self-care as a fundamental aspect of achieving true success and maintaining holistic well-being.

Integrating Self-Care into Daily Routines

Self-care should not be viewed as an occasional indulgence but as a critical component of a daily routine. For Type 3s, integrating self-care practices into their daily schedules ensures that these activities are given the same importance as their professional tasks.

Technique: Start by identifying small self-care actions that can be easily incorporated into your day, such as a ten-minute morning meditation, a midday walk, or an evening gratitude journal. Schedule these activities as non-negotiable appointments in your calendar, reminding yourself that these practices are vital for maintaining your energy and focus.

Mindfulness and Presence

Mindfulness encourages living in the present moment, a practice that can be particularly beneficial for Type 3s, who often focus on future goals and achievements.

Technique: Dedicate time each day to mindfulness practices, such as breathing exercises, guided meditations, or mindful eating. These practices can help you cultivate a sense of presence, reduce stress, and enhance your awareness of your body's needs, leading to improved well-being.

Physical Activity for Stress Relief

Regular physical activity is an effective way to manage stress and improve overall health. For Type 3s, exercise can also provide a productive break from work, offering a sense of accomplishment in a non-work-related context.

Technique: Choose physical activities that you genuinely enjoy, whether it's yoga, running, cycling, or dancing. Viewing exercise as a form of self-care rather than a task or a means to an end can change your relationship with physical activity, making it a joy rather than a chore.

Quality Rest and Sleep

Adequate rest and sleep are foundational for cognitive function, emotional stability, and physical health. Type 3s may struggle to disconnect from their work, affecting their ability to unwind and sleep well.

Technique: Establish a relaxing bedtime routine to signal to your body that it's time to wind down. This might include reading, a warm bath, or gentle stretches. Aim to keep a consistent sleep schedule, even on weekends, to regulate your body's internal clock and improve sleep quality.

Embracing Leisure Without Guilt

Type 3s may feel guilty for taking time off, viewing leisure as unproductive. However, engaging in leisure activities is essential for creativity, relaxation, and personal growth.

Technique: Actively plan leisure activities and hobbies that have no goal other than enjoyment and relaxation. Treat these activities as important for your well-being and personal development. Remember, taking time for leisure is not a sign of laziness but a balanced approach to life.

Type 3 women, adopting a balanced approach to life that includes self-care and relaxation is crucial for sustaining their drive and ambition without succumbing to burnout. By integrating self-care into daily routines, practicing mindfulness, engaging in physical activity, prioritizing rest, and embracing leisure without guilt, Type 3s can support their physical and mental well-being. This chapter not only offers practical techniques for cultivating a healthier lifestyle but also emphasizes the importance of self-care as an integral part of achieving lasting success and fulfillment.

Chapter 4:

Embracing Your Full Potential

Unmasking Your Passions: Exercises to Help You Discover Your Intrinsic Motivations and Passions Beyond External Validation

For Enneagram Type 3 women, the journey towards embracing their full potential often involves peeling away layers of external validation to discover the true passions that ignite their spirit from within. This chapter offers a series of exercises designed to guide Type 3 women in uncovering their intrinsic motivations and passions, fostering a deeper connection to their authentic selves and empowering them to pursue paths that resonate with their core being.

Reflective Journaling

Journaling provides a private, introspective space where Type 3s can explore their thoughts and feelings without the influence of external expectations.

Exercise: Dedicate time each day to journal about what activities make you lose track of time or what you would do if success were guaranteed. Reflect on moments when you felt most alive and fulfilled. Through these reflections, patterns may emerge that highlight your true passions and interests.

Exploring Childhood Interests

Revisiting your childhood can reveal interests and passions that were pursued purely for the joy they brought, untainted by external validation.

Exercise: Create a list of activities you enjoyed as a child or dreamed about doing. Consider how these early interests could be reincorporated into your life now or might inform your current passions and motivations.

Vision Board Creation

A vision board can visually capture your dreams, goals, and desires, serving as a tangible representation of your intrinsic motivations.

Exercise: Gather magazines, photos, quotes, and any other materials that inspire you. Assemble a vision board that reflects your aspirations and passions beyond your achievements. Place it somewhere you will see daily as a reminder of your authentic desires.

Mindfulness and Meditation

Mindfulness practices can help quiet the noise of external expectations, allowing you to connect with your inner voice and true desires.

Exercise: Engage in daily meditation, focusing on your breath or a mantra that resonates with you. Use this time to listen to your inner self, setting aside thoughts of achievement and external validation. Through regular practice, insights into your genuine passions may surface.

Experimentation and Exploration

Trying new activities without the pressure to excel can open doors to discovering passions you were previously unaware of.

Exercise: Make a commitment to try something new each month, whether it's a hobby, class, or experience. Approach these activities with curiosity rather than a goal-oriented mindset, allowing yourself to explore what truly brings you joy and fulfillment.

Seeking Feedback from Trusted Loved Ones

Sometimes, those closest to us can see aspects of ourselves that we overlook, including our genuine passions and strengths.

Exercise: Have conversations with trusted friends or family members about what they perceive as your strengths and interests. Ask them to share instances when they noticed you were genuinely engaged and happy. Their observations can offer valuable insights into your true passions.

Type 3 women, unmasking your passions and connecting with your intrinsic motivations is a crucial step towards embracing your full potential. By engaging in these exercises, Type 3s can embark on a journey of self-discovery that leads to a more authentic and fulfilling life, grounded in passions that resonate deeply with their true selves. This chapter not only provides practical tools for this exploration but also reinforces the importance of looking beyond external validation to uncover the rich tapestry of interests and desires that define who you are at your core.

The Power of Vulnerability and Growth: Techniques for Embracing Your Vulnerabilities as a Source of Strength and Personal Growth

In the journey toward embracing full potential, Enneagram Type 3 women, often admired for their competence, success, and adaptability, face the challenge of acknowledging and embracing their vulnerabilities. Far from being a sign of weakness, vulnerability is a profound source of strength and a catalyst for personal growth. This chapter explores techniques that enable Type 3 women to harness the power of their vulnerabilities, transforming them into opportunities for deeper self-understanding, authentic connections, and sustained personal development.

Acknowledging Vulnerability

The first step in embracing vulnerability is to acknowledge it. For Type 3 women, this can mean recognizing the fears and insecurities that drive their pursuit of success and the facade of infallibility they often feel compelled to maintain.

Technique: Create a private, reflective space for yourself where you can honestly assess your feelings and fears. Writing in a journal can be particularly effective, allowing you to express your vulnerabilities without fear of judgment. Identify specific situations where you feel vulnerable and explore the emotions and thoughts associated with these moments.

Cultivating Self-Compassion

Self-compassion is essential for Type 3 women learning to embrace their vulnerabilities. It involves treating oneself with kindness, understanding, and support, especially in moments of perceived failure or inadequacy.

Technique: Practice mindfulness-based self-compassion exercises. Whenever you catch yourself in self-critical thoughts, pause and offer yourself words of compassion, as you would to a dear friend. Remind yourself that imperfection is part of the human experience and that every individual, regardless of achievement, has vulnerabilities.

Sharing with Trusted Others

Sharing your vulnerabilities with trusted friends, family, or mentors can significantly alleviate the burden of carrying them alone. It opens the door to genuine connections and the discovery that you are not alone in your fears and insecurities.

Technique: Choose a trusted person with whom you feel safe and gradually begin to share your vulnerabilities. Start with smaller disclosures and, as trust builds, allow yourself to share more deeply. Pay attention to the relief and connection that come from being seen and accepted in your entirety.

Transforming Vulnerabilities into Strengths

Vulnerabilities, when acknowledged and embraced, can become powerful sources of strength. They can foster resilience, empathy, and a deeper understanding of oneself and others.

Technique: Reflect on past moments of vulnerability and the outcomes that followed. Often, you'll find that these moments led to personal growth, new perspectives, or strengthened relationships. Use these reflections to reframe how you view vulnerability — not as a weakness but as a conduit for growth and learning.

Setting Boundaries for Vulnerability

While embracing vulnerability is crucial, so is setting boundaries around it. Understanding when and with whom to share your vulnerabilities protects you from potential harm and ensures that your openness leads to positive outcomes.

Technique: Develop an internal gauge for assessing the safety and appropriateness of sharing your vulnerabilities. Consider the trustworthiness of the person, the setting, and your own readiness to be vulnerable. Remember, embracing vulnerability is a choice that should serve your well-being and growth.

Type 3 women, embracing vulnerability is an act of courage that leads to unparalleled personal growth and the realization of their full potential. By acknowledging their vulnerabilities, practicing self-compassion, sharing with trusted others, transforming vulnerabilities into strengths, and setting appropriate boundaries, Type 3s can forge a path of authenticity, resilience, and deep, meaningful success. This chapter not only guides Type 3 women in navigating the complexities of vulnerability but also celebrates it as a cornerstone of true strength and enduring personal achievement.

Chapter 5:

Women and Leadership

Leading with Authenticity: Strategies for Leading with Confidence While Staying True to Your Values and Personality

In the realm of leadership, authenticity stands as a beacon, guiding women to lead with integrity, confidence, and a deep connection to their values and true selves. For Enneagram Type 3 women, known for their adaptability, achievement orientation, and drive for success, the challenge often lies in balancing these qualities with the vulnerability and authenticity required for truly impactful leadership. Drawing upon the wisdom of the Enneagram, this chapter explores strategies for Type 3 women to lead authentically, fostering environments of trust, respect, and mutual growth.

Embrace Your Unique Leadership Style

Authentic leadership begins with self-awareness and an embrace of one's unique leadership style, grounded in personal values and strengths.

Strategy: Reflect on your core values and how they align with your leadership approach. Identify the strengths that you naturally bring to leadership roles, whether it's your ability to motivate others, your strategic thinking, or your capacity for empathy. Emphasize these strengths in your leadership style, rather than conforming to traditional or expected leadership molds.

Cultivate Emotional Intelligence

Emotional intelligence is a cornerstone of authentic leadership, enabling leaders to connect with others deeply, navigate complex interpersonal dynamics, and foster a culture of empathy and understanding.

Strategy: Develop your emotional intelligence by practicing active listening, empathy, and self-regulation. Seek feedback from colleagues and team members on your emotional impact and areas for growth. Incorporate mindfulness practices to enhance your awareness of your own emotions and those of others.

Transparent Communication

Authentic leaders communicate transparently, sharing not only their visions and expectations but also their challenges and uncertainties.

Strategy: Foster an environment of open communication by being honest about both successes and setbacks. Encourage dialogue, share your thought processes, and invite input from others. This transparency builds trust and shows that you value the contributions and perspectives of your team.

Lead by Example

One of the most powerful ways to lead authentically is to model the behaviors and attitudes you wish to see in your team.

Strategy: Demonstrate commitment, integrity, and a strong work ethic. Show vulnerability by admitting mistakes and sharing lessons learned. Your example can inspire others to act with authenticity and courage, creating a ripple effect of positive change within your organization.

Encourage Authenticity in Others

Authentic leadership is not just about being true to oneself; it's also about encouraging others to bring their whole selves to work.

Strategy: Create a supportive environment where diverse perspectives and backgrounds are valued. Celebrate individual contributions that stem from unique experiences and viewpoints. By validating the authenticity of others, you foster a culture of inclusivity and innovation.

Prioritize Self-Reflection and Growth

Authentic leadership is a continuous journey of self-reflection and personal growth. Regularly taking stock of your leadership approach and its alignment with your values is crucial for maintaining authenticity.

Strategy: Set aside time for regular self-reflection, whether through journaling, meditation, or coaching. Reflect on your leadership experiences, the decisions you've made, and how they align with your authentic self. Embrace lifelong learning and growth as integral components of your leadership journey.

Type 3 women, leading with authenticity offers a path to meaningful and effective leadership, characterized by deep connections, mutual respect, and a commitment to personal and collective growth. By embracing their unique leadership style, cultivating emotional intelligence, communicating transparently, leading by example, encouraging authenticity in others, and prioritizing self-reflection, Type 3 women can achieve leadership success that is both impactful and true to their values and personality. This chapter not only provides practical strategies for authentic leadership but also underscores the transformative power of leading with authenticity in cultivating environments where everyone is empowered to achieve their full potential.

Building Strong Teams: Techniques for Fostering Collaboration and Motivation Within Your Team

Type 3 women, who are naturally driven by achievement and success, the ability to build and lead strong, cohesive teams is essential. A successful team is not just about individual excellence but about how well members work together, support each other, and stay motivated towards common goals. This chapter outlines techniques that can help Type 3 women foster collaboration and motivation within their teams, leveraging their leadership skills to create an environment where everyone thrives.

Create a Clear and Compelling Vision

A shared vision is the foundation of a motivated and collaborative team. It provides a common direction and purpose, uniting team members towards a collective goal.

Technique: Involve your team in creating this vision. Host a session where everyone can contribute ideas and define what success looks like for the group. This collaborative approach ensures buy-in and makes the vision more meaningful to each team member.

Leverage Individual Strengths

Understanding and leveraging the unique strengths of each team member not only boosts productivity but also enhances self-esteem and job satisfaction.

Technique: Utilize personality assessments or strength-finding tools to identify the strengths of your team members. Assign roles and tasks based on these strengths, and acknowledge each member's contributions regularly. This personalized approach will make your team feel valued and more invested in the team's success.

Foster Open Communication

Open and honest communication is crucial for collaboration and the resolution of conflicts. As a leader, it's important to model this transparency and encourage it within your team.

Technique: Establish regular team meetings and one-on-one check-ins to ensure open lines of communication. Create a safe space where team members feel comfortable voicing their ideas, concerns, and feedback. Listening actively and empathetically demonstrates your commitment to their well-being and the team's success.

Cultivate a Culture of Trust

Trust is the cornerstone of any strong team. It encourages risk-taking, innovation, and mutual support among team members.

Technique: Lead by example to build trust. Be consistent in your actions and follow through on your promises. Show vulnerability by admitting mistakes and sharing challenges you're facing. Encourage team members to do the same, reinforcing that it's safe to take risks and learn from failures.

Encourage Professional and Personal Growth

Investing in the growth of your team members not only benefits their personal development but also contributes to the team's and organization's success.

Technique: Offer opportunities for professional development, such as workshops, courses, or mentorship programs. Support their personal growth initiatives by recognizing their efforts and celebrating their achievements. Encouraging growth shows your investment in their future and motivates them to contribute their best to the team.

Celebrate Team Achievements

Recognizing and celebrating achievements reinforces a sense of accomplishment and unity. It motivates the team to continue working towards their goals with enthusiasm.

Technique: Celebrate both big wins and small milestones. Use team meetings to highlight achievements, thank individuals for their contributions, and share how each success brings the team closer to its overall vision. These celebrations can boost morale and foster a strong sense of community within the team.

Enneagram Type 3 women in leadership roles, building strong teams is a dynamic and ongoing process that requires attention to the individual and collective needs of team members. By creating a clear vision, leveraging individual strengths, fostering open communication, cultivating trust, encouraging growth, and celebrating achievements, Type 3 leaders can inspire collaboration and motivation. These strategies not only enhance team performance but also align with the authentic leadership style of Type 3 women, allowing them to lead with confidence while staying true to their values and personality.

Chapter 6:

Exploring Your Wings

Understanding the Influences of Type Four and Type Two: A Section Dedicated to Exploring How the Wings (Type 3w4 and Type 3w2) Influence Personality, Strengths, and Challenges of Threes

Enneagram Type 3 women, celebrated for their ambition, adaptability, and focus on achievement, are significantly influenced by their adjacent types or "wings." These wings, Type Four (The Individualist) and Type Two (The Helper), enrich the Type 3 personality with additional layers of complexity, strengths, and challenges. This chapter delves into how these wings manifest in Type 3 women, impacting their motivations, behavior patterns, and paths to personal growth.

Type 3w4: The Professional Individualist

Type 3s with a Four wing (3w4) blend the achievement-oriented focus of Type 3 with the self-awareness and depth of Type Four. This combination creates a unique profile of a professional who is not only driven to succeed but also deeply values authenticity and individual expression.

Strengths: The 3w4 subtype excels in environments where success and uniqueness are both valued. They possess a creative flair in their pursuits, often bringing innovative solutions to the table. Their work is marked by a personal touch, distinguishing them from their peers. Additionally, the introspective nature of the Four wing allows them to connect with others on a meaningful level, enhancing their leadership with empathy and understanding.

Challenges: The main challenge for 3w4s lies in balancing their need for achievement with their desire for authenticity. They may struggle with feelings of inadequacy or inauthenticity, particularly in highly competitive environments. The introspective nature of the Four wing can also lead to periods of self-doubt, impacting their typically high levels of productivity and confidence.

Strategies for Growth: Embrace your unique blend of ambition and individualism. Pursue projects that allow you to express your creativity and authenticity. Practice self-compassion and remind yourself that your worth is not solely tied to your achievements or how distinctively you present your work.

Type 3w2: The Charismatic Helper

Type 3s with a Two wing (3w2) integrate the drive and goal-oriented nature of Type 3 with the caring, people-focused qualities of Type Two. This synthesis produces a charismatic leader who not only aims for success but also places a high value on relationships and helping others.

Strengths: 3w2s are natural networkers, skilled at building and maintaining relationships. Their ability to connect with people, combined with their ambition, often propels them into leadership roles where they can motivate and inspire their teams. The Two wing enhances their empathetic understanding, enabling them to lead with compassion and genuine concern for the well-being of their colleagues and subordinates.

Challenges: The 3w2 subtype may find it challenging to maintain boundaries, as their desire to be liked and to help can sometimes overshadow their own needs and priorities. They may also struggle with the balance between achieving their goals and the time and energy spent supporting others, potentially leading to burnout.

Strategies for Growth: Focus on developing healthy boundaries and learning to say no when necessary. Prioritize your goals and recognize that being supportive does not require sacrificing your ambitions. Cultivate self-awareness to understand when your actions are driven by a genuine desire to help versus a need for approval.

Enneagram Type 3 women, understanding the nuances of their wings—whether leaning towards the introspective and authentic aspects of the Four or the relational and altruistic traits of the Two—provides invaluable insights into their complex personalities. Embracing the strengths and addressing the challenges of their wings can empower Type 3s to lead with authenticity, build strong relationships, and achieve success that resonates deeply with their values and sense of self. This chapter not only explores the dynamics of these influences but also offers strategies for personal and professional growth, enabling Type 3 women to fully embrace their potential and lead with confidence and integrity.

Growth and Integration: Moving Towards Health

Enneagram Type 3 women, celebrated for their adaptability, ambition, and focus on achievement, encounter unique pathways of growth and challenges. Understanding how Type 3s integrate towards Type Six in moments of growth and disintegrate towards Type Nine under stress is crucial for their personal development and well-being. This section examines these dynamics and provides strategies for managing these movements, encouraging Type 3 women to navigate their journey with awareness and resilience.

Integration Towards Type Six: The Loyalist

In growth, Type 3s move towards the positive aspects of Type Six, embracing qualities such as loyalty, reliability, and a strong sense of community. This movement signifies a shift from an emphasis on personal achievement to a recognition of the importance of trust, security, and mutual support.

Characteristics of Growth: As Type 3s integrate towards Type Six, they become more team-oriented, valuing collaboration and the collective success over individual accolades. They show a heightened awareness of potential risks and a more cautious approach to decision-making, balancing their natural assertiveness with careful planning and consideration of others' viewpoints.

Strategies for Integration:

Cultivate Trust: Focus on building deeper, trust-based relationships with colleagues, friends, and family. Be consistent in your actions and follow through on commitments.

Seek Feedback: Openly solicit feedback from others to gain diverse perspectives and demonstrate your investment in the team or community's collective success.

Embrace Teamwork: Actively participate in group activities and projects, valuing the process of collaboration as much as the outcome.

Disintegration Towards Type Nine: The Peacemaker

Under stress, Type 3s may exhibit characteristics associated with Type Nine, retreating from their goal-oriented nature to adopt a more passive and complacent stance. This shift often manifests as avoiding conflict, minimizing personal needs and desires, and disengaging from their ambitions.

Characteristics of Stress: In times of stress, Type 3s might find themselves procrastinating, downplaying their achievements, and seeking comfort in routine or familiar tasks. There's a tendency to prioritize peace and harmony at the expense of their own progress and authentic self-expression.

Strategies for Managing Stress:

Acknowledge Your Feelings: Recognize when you're avoiding conflict or disengaging due to stress. Acknowledge your feelings instead of pushing them aside.

Set Small, Achievable Goals: When overwhelmed, break down tasks into smaller, manageable goals to avoid inertia and re-engage with your ambition in a balanced way.

Practice Mindfulness: Engage in mindfulness exercises to stay connected with your present experiences and feelings, reducing the urge to retreat or disengage.

Enneagram Type 3 women, the journey of personal growth involves navigating the balance between their natural drive for achievement and the need for connection, trust, and stability. By embracing the qualities of Type Six in moments of growth and effectively managing the stress-induced tendencies towards Type Nine, Type 3s can achieve a more fulfilled and balanced life. This chapter not only outlines the dynamics of these movements but also offers practical strategies for integration and stress management, empowering Type 3 women to lead a life that truly resonates with their deepest values and aspirations.

CHAPTER 7:

WORKBOOK

Did you love *The woman of Enneagram 3: Love marriage success edition*? Then you should read *The woman of Enneagram 1: Love Marriage Success Edition*[1] by Maria Rondon!

Enneagram Type 1 Woman: Unleash Your Inner Perfection (Enneagram Book, Enneagram for Adult Women)

Discover the transformative power of the Enneagram as a Type 1 woman. This life-changing book provides invaluable insights into the core motivations, strengths, and growth opportunities for the Perfectionist personality type.

As an Enneagram Type 1, you strive for excellence, order, and integrity in all aspects of life. While these qualities are admirable, they can also lead to self-criticism, rigid thinking, and a fear of making

1. https://books2read.com/u/mvMrye

2. https://books2read.com/u/mvMrye

mistakes. This book empowers you to embrace your true essence while breaking free from limiting patterns.

Through thought-provoking exercises and real-life examples, you'll explore how the Enneagram impacts your relationships (Enneagram in Love, Enneagram in Marriage), career, and personal growth journey. Gain a deeper understanding of your drives, learn to temper your inner critic, and develop self-compassion and balance.

Whether you're seeking to improve your relationships, advance in your career, or simply live a more authentic and fulfilling life, this book is a powerful guide. It offers practical strategies and insights to help you harness the strengths of your Type 1 personality while addressing your core fears and blind spots.

Dive into this life-changing book today and embark on a journey of self-discovery, personal empowerment (Enneagram Empowerment), and profound growth (Enneagram for Personal Growth). Unlock your true potential as an Enneagram Type 1 woman and live with greater presence, purpose, and inner peace.

Also by Maria Rondon

Alzheimer
Alzheimer Guia para cuidadores

Enneagram For Women
The woman of Enneagram 1: Love Marriage Success Edition
The woman of enneagram 2
The woman of Enneagram 3: Love marriage success edition
The Woman of Enneagram 4: Love, Marriage, Success Edition
The woman of Enneagram 5: Love marriage success edition
The Woman of Enneagram 6: Love, Marriage, Success Edition
The woman of Enneagram 7: Love marriage success edition
The woman of Enneagram 8: Love marriage success edition
The woman of Enneagram 9: Love marriage success edition

LOA
El secreto para atraer tu alma gemela